How to Run a Successful B&B

Secrets from an Award-winning B&B Owner

ANGELA CAMPBELL

Cartoons by Rik

Copyright © 1999 Angela Campbell

No part of this publication may be reproduced, stored in a retrieval system, or transmitted in any form or by any means, electronic, mechanical, photocopying, recording, or otherwise without the prior permission of the author.

All rights reserved.
ISBN-10: 1548821217
ISBN-13: 978-1548821210

First published 1999
Revised 2001, 2003 and 2017
Reprinted January 2007 and 2017
2nd Edition

Publisher: Harbour Lookout Publishing
5 Mount Boone, Dartmouth, Devon TQ6 9PB
Tel: 01803 833438
campbelldartmouth@yahoo.com

www.campbellsbb.com
Copies of this book are available from the publisher and on Amazon.

All rights reserved. Although every effort has been made to ensure accuracy of the regulations, these are by no means definitive.

A reference to any person, living or dead, is purely coincidental. If there is a Sybil Whatsit of Dunroamin out there who takes offence, please accept a thousand snivelling apologies from the author who really doesn't mean you any harm.

This book is dedicated to Angie's memory.

CONTENTS

ABOUT THE BOOK i
1: THINKING ABOUT IT 1
2: GETTING STARTED 5
3: MARKETING & ADVERTISING 13
4: THE TOURIST INFORMATION CENTRE 21
5: GETTING THEM ACROSS THE DOORMAT 26
6: WHAT ELSE TO PROVIDE 34
7: MONEY, MONEY 42
8: YOU CAN'T PLEASE ALL THE FOLK ALL THE TIME 48
ABOUT THE AUTHOR 53

ABOUT THE BOOK

B&B may sound like a great idea. But how do you turn that dream into reality? Is it really as simple as it seems? Where do you start? What about planning permission and regulations and whatever else Brussels has thought up to stop a citizen making an honest crust? What about advertising? How about evening meals? How much should you charge and what can you expect to make in a good year?

This book provides most of the answers.

Written in humorous chatty style with tales from the author's extensive experience, it's packed with tips and ideas on how to set up and run a successful B&B.

It won't tell you how to do B&B because that's up to you; after all, it's your home and how you treat guests is your business. Nor will it tell you how to fry an egg – let's leave that to Delia – but it will reveal how the author does it successfully and how to avoid some of the pitfalls. It will save you money and it may help to maximise your potential.

"Informative and amusing. Essential for those who want to get it right from the start"

1: THINKING ABOUT IT

So, you think it will be rather nice to earn a bit of pin money doing B&B? Tommy's just gone off to university and his room isn't being used, so why not hang out a sign and earn a few quid in term time. After all, Mrs Whatsit down the road does it and she seems to do all right; bet she doesn't put all those tenners through the books (nudge, nudge, wink, wink – know what I mean?) Perhaps your old man is coming up for retirement and you've always thought it would be fun to buy a little guest house in Seamouth; nice little earner to pad out the pension. You could do the breakfasts and then spend the rest of the day lazing on the beach and eating cream teas like you did last hols. Or maybe you've had it up to here with the rat race and want to have a complete break: Bury yourself in the country and work from home; start the Good Life with a few chickens and a cow; the missus could do a bit of B&B with evening meals; she's always been quite a good cook.

So let's assume you've never done this sort of thing before but you'd like to give it a try. Perhaps the first thing you should decide is why? Do you want to make a living out of this? Do you want to make a few bob to pay for the holidays? Or are you just in need of company? For whatever reason, it's perhaps worth knowing a couple of home truths about the business. I don't want to put you off, but you should have a pretty good idea about what it could entail before you hang out that sign. And it doesn't make a jot of difference whether you have a palace on Park Lane or a semi by the sea, the downside is just the same. So, let's grasp a few nettles right away.

THE DOWNSIDE

It can involve a lot of your time. When you see a hotel owner beaming benignly at his guests, it may seem that he's having a whale of a time throwing a dinner party every night. What you don't see is him eating his main meal at two in the morning after all the washing up, grabbing a few hours' sleep before getting up to do the breakfasts at seven, then starting the whole day all over again with the plastic smile welded permanently to his face. The B&B owner is no different, especially if the house is going to be kept mother-in-law-clean and you're staying on top of the laundry while the guests are out there enjoying the summer sun; while they play, you work. And then you might have to wait around for guests who may or may not, turn up at the door, or tie yourself to the Talking Bone in case someone calls with a booking.

If you think you'll make your fortune, forget it and don't give up the day job. Generally, the more beds the better, but you're unlikely to make a decent living out of B&B unless you have at least six bedrooms.

And you won't start rolling in riches right away. If you're starting from scratch, the business will take time to build. The received wisdom of small business management is that you keep it the first year, it keeps itself the second and starts to keep you in the third; it's unlikely to really get going for a few years.

The place will never be the same again. Notices, fire extinguishers, smoke alarms, locks on the bedroom doors; the list goes on. Snores coming through the wall. And strangers wandering around your home poking into cupboards and asking for milk just as you've settled down to watch your favourite programme on the telly.

And then there's the expense. Let's face it, you have to spend money to make it. Are you prepared to make major alterations like the installation of bathrooms, and cope with complying with all those Euroregs?

Of course, they don't have to be done at once; you can do them as you go along and a smart accountant will be able to use some of them to offset tax. You may have to take on extra help to cope with the cleaning and laundry.

What about kids and pets and smokers and incontinent grannies? Well, you'll have to decide on those for yourself. Actually, it's not that bad because, on the whole, they're usually on their best behaviour in a stranger's house.

Still interested? Great. But hang in there because there is one more – very important – point of principle which you need to decide upon before we progress. Are you going to play at this, or are you prepared to treat it as a business with all the commitment that entails? There are people who fiddle with it: they're the ones who open up just to take advantage of the high season; they're the ones who don't really care what customers want; they're the ones who just take the money and run; and they're quite often the ones who give this business a tacky, downmarket image that it doesn't deserve.

THE UPSIDE

Still with me? Fine. If I haven't put you off completely, pop off and have a beer because there definitely is an upside. If you like people, you will certainly meet a lot of them; they come as guests and leave as friends, and some come back again. They tell their friends and they come too. It may take some time; let's face it, they may have plans to holiday on the Costa Del Plonk next year.

The money will be there. Even with one letting bedroom you can make quite a few quid right away and you can pad that out by doing evening meals; every day is payday. The more you put into it, the more will come back. From little acorns, great oaks grow; the business will expand and, in next to no time, you'll be a real B&B enthusiast like the rest of us.

CHIPS

Suzie was our first helper in the restaurant. Suzie was Scots, ruddily rotund, slightly rough round the edges, and absolutely agricultural. But she had previously worked in a restaurant and we hadn't, so Suzie was gold dust.

We had determined that this was going to be an up-market restaurant, but we hadn't reckoned on the Suzie factor. When one of our first diners had the temerity to request chips, Suzie drew herself up to her full four feet two, set full sail and bustled out, declaring in broadest Aberdonian, 'Chips? We don't serve chips in MY restaurant!'

2: GETTING STARTED

There are several different types of B&B: hotel, boutique, guest house, or traditional rooms in a home. What's in a name? In the UK, there's no difference between guest house, boutique or B&B, it's largely a matter of individual perception; in New Zealand, a B&B can mean self-catering and home-stay is just exactly that.

Where do you want to start? Do you want to kick off from scratch as I did, or do you want to take over an existing business? What experience do you have of catering and small businesses, and how committed do you want to be? Wherever, be it an artisan B&B or a commercial mini-hotel, the philosophy for success is just the same.

TAKING OVER AN EXISTING BUSINESS

There are a myriad of reasons why a business comes on the market. If you're lucky, you can just put down your suitcases, take over the bookings and start making money. We sold our wee hotel with a cracking reputation, but the new owners ran it into the ground within months. We stayed in one B&B because it had a top-quality rating, but it soon became evident that the owners had inherited the rating and their standards fell far short of the mark. If there's any doubt, it's worth doing some basic research into the past before you start: what sort of reputation did it have; was there any history of problems, etc. If so, the received wisdom is to advertise that it's under new management. Or simply change the name.

STARTING FROM SCRATCH

So, let's assume that you're starting with rooms in your house and have never done this before. Perhaps the first thing to realise is that there's a lot of advice available and it's mainly free: Government agencies and the local council are keen to develop tourism; Tourist Information Centres are always looking for new blood; and other B&B owners are usually very happy to share their experiences with you.

MARKET RESEARCH

Market research may sound a baffling buzzword from the city slickers. It doesn't always require masses of graphs, guesstimates and computer graphics. Actually, it's basic common sense to find out how much demand there is for B&B in your area, what the going rate is and how much competition there is out there. You can do this quite easily by visiting your local friendly Tourist Information Centre (TIC). They'll be only too happy to answer your questions. They've got a pretty good feel for the demand, the season, and what the market is prepared to pay. They will also be able to advise you about the current Quality Grading scheme and whether registration is required; some TICs have a policy to only accept establishments that are graded. More about this later.

THE DISTRICT COUNCIL

The next stop should be the District Council. They're very willing to help because they want to ensure that folk are aware of the regulations. They're not Big Brothers; just because you ask for advice, they're not going to come sneaking round in the middle of the night to see if you're breaking the rules and drag you off in front of the magistrates. If they're aware that you want to get things right from the outset, they'll be very happy to advise.

Visit the Planning Department. Explain that you'r starting a B&B and ask about planning requirements change of use. The six-bed rule may apply. Basically that if six or fewer souls sleep in the house – ex the proprietors – you may not need to register for change of use or business rates. These regulations may change from one local authority to the next.

Then talk to Environmental Health. Anyone who supplies food for guests must register with their local authority at least 28 days prior to trading. They want to ensure that you don't poison anyone who eats in your esteemed establishment. They will require you to hold a Level 2 Award in Food Safety and Catering. This means that you have to pay for a four-hour training session, followed by a simple multiple-choice exam. Did you know that you can't keep cleaning chemicals under the kitchen sink, or that you have to have five different preparation mats, or that wooden chopping boards are a no-no? Of course you did, but you still have to have a certificate to prove it. Then the Environmental Health inspector will need to pay you a visit. One female inspecting another's kitchen? Oh my Lord! However, they're very tactful and will probably send you on a wee errand while she runs her hands over the work surfaces and peeks in the fridge. Ideally, you should have a separate fridge for the B&B food, but she'll probably be quite happy if you keep the bacon and sausages in a dedicated drawer of your domestic one.

Another body worth consulting is the Fire Station. They will advise on how to conduct a Fire Risk Self Assessment. And also what you will need in the way of sensors, signs, extinguishers and exits so that everyone can get out within 2.5 minutes; it's OK for you to fry but not the paying punter.

Alternatively, do an internet search for Do You Have Paying Guests? ISBN 9781409805311, a government publication.

OTHERS WHO'LL NEED TO KNOW

Mortgage companies are sometimes a bit prickly about conducting business from what they perceive to be their properties; we once had to change our lender because of this.

Your house insurance company will also want to know, especially when it comes to Public Liability and Fire and Theft cover; they may decline to offer accidental damage cover for contents. You may have to pay an increased premium, but it's worth the peace of mind to have proper cover. Many proprietors don't bother, but just imagine the ramifications of a fire-related death to a paying guest if you don't have cover.

Your car premiums may go up by a tenner or so when you tell them that you're conducting a business, even popping down to the Cash and Carry. Insurance companies are the first to go slopey-shouldered and refuse to pay if they can wriggle out of it. One hotelier we knew had a fire and wanted to make a few alterations in the rebuilding. His insurance company insisted that he put everything back just the way it was before the fire. It was only after he pointed out that one wall was constructed of dung and horse hair that they relented. Another hotelier had payment refused because they claimed the owner was over-insured. You can't win, but you can avoid most of the hassle by being open with them.

It's a good idea to think about consulting an accountant at this stage. I know it's early days yet and you're not even sure the business will take off, and accountants are expensive and all the other arguments. Believe me, my old man's such a rabid Scot that he won't use a first-class stamp except in dire emergency, but even he suggested using an accountant right away. Shop around: ask other small business owners who they use; ask accountants what experience they have with small businesses, and what their rates are. I keep my own trading accounts and my yearly bill is only three room-nights. More on this later, but the value of consulting at this stage is that you will know the best way to lay out your trading accounts. Also, he will advise about what is, or is not, allowable against tax; you can save quite a lot by starting with secondhand equipment and upgrading once the money starts to roll in.

Some local authorities and tourist boards give grants to upgrade establishments – installing en-suite bathrooms is a favourite. It really boils down to tourism demand and how much money's in the pot when you make an application. They will probably require three estimates for the work – just try getting one out of your average country tradesman, let alone three. Also, horror of horrors, a business plan. We had to cobble one of those together in Scotland. A nice man at the grants office came all the way out from Edinburgh and made it up for us, pulling guesstimates out of the air at random. It worked and we got our grant, but then found that we were tied to continue trading for six years. We got round that by asking the buyer of our hotel to take over stewardship of the grant, which she was quite happy to do because it cost nothing other than a commitment to continue trading.

LICENCES

Can we ever live without them?

TV. If you have these in the bedrooms (and guests now expect them) or anywhere else for the public to view, your regular TV licence isn't enough. Even if you're over the age of 75 you'll need a Hotel and Mobile Units Television Licence (hotel licence) which costs the same as the domestic one. Call 0300 790 6016.

DVDs. It's really hospitable to have a library for guests to use. But, guess what, you need a licence for those, too. Costs about £25-£40. Visit www.filmbank.co.uk.

Music. If you want to play background muzak, you may need a licence from the Performing Rights Society (PRS) to legally play copyrighted music. Don't disregard their first polite request; they hang in there like a mother-in-law in attack mode. B&Bs with fewer than four bedrooms are exempt. A point to beware: two rooms joined by an open door/arch count as one. Costs depend on circumstances, but are about £60. Call 0800 068 4828.

Alcohol. If you're thinking of selling booze, it will be a good idea to check the requirements with the Clerk to the Justices at your local magistrates' court. Liquor licences can be an absolute nightmare if you don't get it right from the start. And, again, regulations may vary from area to area. For example, my local clerk revealed that I can't get any sort of licence with fewer than six to eight letting bedrooms; and that if I bought wine for dinner guests and let them have it at cost, or gave it away as a loss-leader, it would constitute a sale.

Employment. Being an employer is an absolute minefield of regulations, to be avoided if you're an artisan. Just don't.

All this can become very complicated, can't it? I'm a firm believer in the KISS principle. Don't get excited fellas, it stands for Keep It Simple Stupid: I don't play muzak; I don't sell booze; I'm not an employer. And I keep paper records; the battery doesn't go flat on my pencil!

I DON'T LIKE THIS AT ALL

When we turned our home into a licensed restaurant, we had worked very hard to get things right with a barrow-load of bureaucrats. One of the first on the scene was the man who doubled as the building and health inspector. At first sight he was pessimism personified, so we anticipated that the battle was to get him across the threshold and on our side.

'We'd really appreciate your advice,' we said. He melted just a little bit. Then he smelled the freshly brewed coffee and tried my homemade ginger bread and he started to get quite enthusiastic about the whole project. The more we got into him, the more helpful he became and he was soon trying his best to suggest ways of getting round the regulations.

The next major hurdle was a booze licence. My old man went up to the Sheriff's Court with the plans and came up against a seemingly immovable bureaucratic block. The court clerk had returned from holiday and she was just busting to show everyone that she was back in charge. 'I don't like this,' she declared, all huff and puff and officiousness, 'I don't like this at all, and I'm not even going to pass it on to the Sheriff.' The old man returned home in dark despair. Without a liquor licence the whole project couldn't even start.

Then I had a brainwave. 'The health inspector's on our side,' I said, 'let's set him on to that bossy besom; he'll sort her out.' Within an hour of our call to him, she was on the phone positively grovelling with apologetic helpfulness. We were back on track. Just goes to prove that, next to sex appeal, the quickest way to a bureaucrat's heart is through his tum.

But, don't quote me on that.

3: MARKETING & ADVERTISING

Forgive me if this insults your intelligence, but there's a definite difference between the two. Marketing involves pitching your business towards the sort of folk you want to host, and advertising is telling them that you're in business. For example, commercial whiz kids will benefit by attracting business guests, while artisans might prefer tourists or dog-lovers or walkers or grannies.

Advertising can be one of the greatest expenditures because it's very much hit-and-miss; more miss-and-miss if you're not careful. They say that 50% of advertising is effective. But which 50%? And it also usually requires careful selection.

So where do you start? The best analogy is the stone in the pond; chuck one in and watch the ripples spread out. You're the centre of the universe, so start thinking about advertising as close to that centre as possible. And where is that? Right outside your door, that's where it is.

THE SIGN

I only have a discrete sign containing the name, which I prop up on the gate for guests' final guidance. It's not because I'm so successful that I don't need one (wouldn't that be just great?) but because my B&B is not in guest-house alley.

The Planning Department can advise you about the need for consent and the regulations about illumination. If you want one of those white-on-brown signs by the road, consult the Highways Department; it costs about £180.

Whether you're thinking of one to hang outside or just a simple sign in the window, the principles are the same. Back to market research here and another good buzz phrase: TLC – Think Like Customers. TIC and TLC. Gets a bit confusing doesn't it? Stick with me, you'll soon get the hang of it.

What are they looking for as they cruise by in their cars? Take a good look at the other signs in your neighbourhood.

Name. This may sound a bit chichi and there's nothing wrong with Dunroamin, is there? The establishment name is surprisingly important, especially when they're selecting your B&B from a brochure or the internet. People rather like the feeling of staying in an old, established place: The Old Vicarage, Bake House, Grange, Rectory, Lodge, Cottage all go down well; and a name that contains heavy consonants – Longbow Barns, for example – has a good solid historical ring to it.

Facilities. Besides B&B, what other information is needed on a sign? My first one just stated B&B Good Food. My old man thought it was a bit pretentious but it brought home the bacon. A trap to beware: some folk cram so much information onto a board that it's barely readable, certainly at 30mph as the customers whizz down the road. Certain items, like en-suite bathrooms, parking and TV may catch the eye, but who is really drawn by central heating in summer?

Quality grading symbols, the more the merrier, may sway the customer towards your door. Colour can be eye-catching – black on yellow used to be the 'in' combination – but how much more appealing is a hand-painted sign in comfortable colours?

A No Vacancies supplementary sign can be useful; even if you're not full, there will be times when you just don't want anyone in the house.

The Tourist Information Centre will probably run two schemes: simple adverts on a board in the Centre and a glossy brochure entitled Where to Stay, or some such. They both cost – what doesn't nowadays? – but they will probably bring in the bulk of your business at the start, especially if you're close to the centre of their universe. After five years trading, the TIC and their Where to Stay brochure used to bring in 60% of my bookings, but the internet is beginning to be more effective.

FREE, GRATIS AND FOR NOTHING

The best form of advertising is word of mouth. It costs absolutely nothing and is worth a hundred glossy brochures. Your friends will tell their friends and Mrs Whatsit down the road will pass on some of her overflow and so on; it's a good ploy to invite other B&B owners round for coffee (or something stronger) and offer to reciprocate with bookings. Once you get going, your guests will be so overwhelmed by the quality of your esteemed establishment that they'll shout the good news from the rooftops, won't they? Even after four years, word of mouth will probably bring in fewer than 40% of the bookings. Eventually it may rise to 100%. But 'eventually' is that place just over the horizon, so take out your credit card, crunch your teeth and stand by to spend money in order to make it.

You can get a free entry in Yell. Call 0800 533 433 or visit www.yell.com.

National newspaper and magazine articles can be worth twice their weight in gold.

I stress national because local can be a waste of money unless it's a result of getting awards. They are essentially ephemeral but they can last a surprisingly long time. A journalist wrote an article about me in Figaro, a yuppie magazine in Japan. After the initial burst of interest, I thought it had gone the way of most magazines – into file 13. But four years later, Japanese guests were faxing from Osaka and turning up at the door clutching that torn-out page from Figaro.

NEARLY FREE

If you are looking for B&B where would you ask, besides the TIC and the internet? A simple flyer in the pub, the local shop and the filling station can work wonders.

HANDBOOKS AND GUIDES

Handbooks on where to stay are a bit of a lottery, not least because there are so many of them. One guest house owner I know takes advertising space in every one he can find in the bookshop, and he swears by them. However, I suspect that he doesn't really analyse the effectiveness of his advertising and he must spend two small fortunes taking all those entries.

If you can identify a niche market – Toy Poodle Breeders Anonymous, or whatever – entries in handbooks or magazines which service that market can produce good results.

Clubmanship can also work in your favour; an entry headed Members' B&B, or Retired Employees Home in a company House magazine is worth considering, and they're usually inexpensive.

Practically all of them take it from both sides, from you and advertisers, and charges are rarely less than three room-nights. Beware the early-season phone call, trying to get you to buy space. They're usually accompanied by frantic typing in the background. 'We've just got a few spaces left, Mrs Whatsit, and we can offer you a full-page for only £3,000.99, plus VAT.' You'll probably find it's Bald-Headed Banjo Players Weekly and will bring in precisely the square root of absolutely nothing. The same goes for adverts in the daily press, which are so ephemeral that they're only useful for tearing up and hanging on a nail in the privy.

It's worth asking a few pertinent questions about their market and distribution, and ask for a copy to prove your entry. What is certain is that they'll be back time and again asking you to take more entries.

BUSINESS CARDS AND BROCHURES

Cards are absolutely essential and need not be very expensive, especially if you can design your own on the computer; not just for putting in bedrooms but also that casual conversation in the pub.
A card with a picture on one side and limited wording on the other will not be thrown away quite as quickly as others; the hope is that folk will flash them around like holiday snaps. I have mine printed

the size of a credit card. On the reverse is the simple summary of my facilities, including contact details and website.

A picture is worth a thousand words, whether it's a photo or a lithograph. The great advantage of both is that you can subtly edit out undesirable features, like telephone poles and trees, without falling foul of Truth in Advertising. Most advertisers expect a pretty picture, so it's worth getting good quality shots of the house or view, whatever you feel can be beneficial. Holiday accommodation is usually chosen by the ladies who want to see at least a picture of the bedrooms. A shot of the house showing an open (welcome) door, preferably with smiling people entering or leaving, gives a nice warm glow. It almost goes without saying that external shots should be taken in National Geographic sunshine, so it may take some time to build a library.

Brochures are more expensive; they can typically cost about £1.30 each for a run of 100. I tend not to order more because details can change; I leave the price blank and write that in after agreeing it with the guest. My watchword is Quality; I like to hit 'em with that right from the start, so I use 300gm Silk Art Paper with lots of pretty pictures and post it in Conqueror envelopes. However, the website has largely superseded the need for these.

WEBSITE

This is effectively a modern brochure. It costs less per unit and you save on the postage; balm to the old man's Scottish heart. This is the way to go. I've tried it for a year and it's wiped its face; it's generated enough bookings to more than pay for a professional firm to design and update the site. But it's not just all that the marketing boys would have us believe. It largely depends on the customers' ability to search. I tried searching for ours under B&B Dartmouth; up came three pages of Dartmouth USA before it got to us. An effective but reasonably inexpensive bolt-on is to buy a link to your site from others – the TIC, for example.

INTERNET BOOKING

Fast-lane folk may find this a convenient way to book but it ain't necessarily so. We don't have it because it may mean handing over your booking diary to the computer with obvious hazards.

We prefer to sell ourselves over the phone. This business is essentially one of personal contact; quick convenience is fine, but there's nothing quite like a cheery chat to project one's personality. The optimum combination can be to take the reservation online and follow it with a telephone call in which you can cover a lot of details quickly.

Another potential problem occurs when more than one agency handles your diary. Double bookings can occur as they both gain access; I get a few referrals from other B&B owners as a result.

Most agencies charge up to 20%. Airbnb are really good, not least because they only charge about 3%; they take the rest from the guests in 'administration fees.' Once you've got through the minefield of registration, they're extremely efficient. I get five emails per booking: Mrs Whatsit wants to book, Mrs Whatsit's booked, Don't forget Mrs Whatsit's coming, Mrs Whatsit's money's in the bank, and Mrs Whatsit's written a report on you, please write one on her before you can view it.

And they do have a helpful customer service where you can talk to a real person in delightful Dublin.

OTHER IDEAS

Postcards. You might think that these are going out of fashion in this increasingly e-world but it's still thriving, especially for holiday-makers. I've taken the photo from my business card and had it printed in postcard size. On the back is printed *The view from Campbells B&B, Dartmouth,* and my website details. I leave one in each room as a freebie. (Come on, Colin, it's good advertising and it only costs pennies!) 'This is for you; send it to Uncle Basil and Aunt Sybil to make them jealous.'

TripAdvisor is an increasingly useful research tool for checking places before booking, so feedback from guests is very important. Yes, I know what some folk say about hosts writing their own glowing report and competitors rubbishing your esteemed establishment. But don't be put off. When guests enthuse about you as they leave (and of course they will), drop a subtle hint in their shell-like to tell TripAdvisor. I've found that their Business Listing doesn't bring any business.

ANALYSIS

Next to waste and staff costs, advertising can run away with the shekels quicker than the tax man. Try it and see is a good maxim, but the only effective result is money in your hot and sticky hand.
I make a note in the booking book where guests heard of us. At the end of the year, I run a simple analysis to check – not so much where they heard of us – but where they did not; and those are the advertisers who are left off the list next year.

THE MACDONALD

In Scotland, we advertised in a small magazine for expats. It was one of those deals where you buy a block of space and fill it with as much as you can. There were a few lines left so my old man said, tongue in cheek, 'How about MacDonalds are welcome; please contact Mrs Campbell?'

Just in case your Scottish history is a bit rusty, the feud between the Campbells and the MacDonalds goes back to 1692 and is second only to the Loch Ness monster in relevance to reality. My old man reckons that MacDonalds are just fine, with mustard. We got quite a few bookings from folk who saw the joke; even had a delightful MacDonald to stay who was a retired policeman, teaching Gaelic in Kent.

But then came the letter from a biddy in Perthshire. 'In view of what your clan did to the MacDonalds in Glencoe, I doubt very much if any member of this illustrious clan would darken your doorstep, let alone accept your hospitality. I speak as a Scotswoman whose mother-in-law's forbears, MacDonalds, were forced to leave their beloved glen and settle in Nova Scotia because of the brutality of your forbears.'

We reckoned that if the letter was written in jest it was funny; if meant seriously, it was hilarious.

ROOM-NIGHTS

It depends on your accounting philosophy. I find it helps to rationalise costs by relating them to room-nights; for example £100 = 1 room-night. When you consider that a four-month season with two bedrooms has a potential of 224 room-nights at £100 per room, you've paid for all that advertising in no time at all. You have to spend money to make it and a smart accountant will be able to use all the appropriate costs to reduce your tax bill.

INDEX CARDS

When we had our restaurant, every host would have an index card. It recorded details of when they dined and any particular likes or dislikes; the cards were filed in a box for future use. The information was really useful. One guest returned after a year and challenged us to remember his previous visit. He was somewhat gobsmacked when I replied, 'How was your visit to London, and would you like your steak medium rare again?' I use a similar system in our B&B.

4: THE TOURIST INFORMATION CENTRE

How does it work? A typical TIC will be open during the summer season. The staff may be paid by the local council or they may run it as their own business. It may be run by a larger Tourist Board or be a member of one. Broadly, the Area board is responsible for collecting and disseminating data about visitor numbers and nationalities; this all helps towards generating funds from Central and European governments.

The TIC income is derived from registration and advertising from the members, plus booking fees from guests. They act as agents for the members – B&B establishments, self-catering and hotels – who are registered with them. As such, they will probably have a policy of not recommending any one establishment, and will leave the customer to select their preference.

A customer looking for accommodation may be shown the display boards and will select, let's say, Mrs Whatsit at Dunroamin. The staff will have made up a list of weekly or daily room availability supplied by the hosts. A call to Mrs Whatsit will confirm that a room is available at the advertised price; if that doesn't work, the staff will ring around other establishments until they can make a reservation.

A Guest Registration Form is completed which records the customer's name, Dunroamin's address and telephone number, directions and the agreed rate. A commission, typically 10% of the first-night's stay, is paid to the TIC; that will be deducted when they settle up with Mrs Whatsit, so the service effectively costs the customer nothing. On arrival at Dunroamin, they hand over one copy, which is retained by Mrs Whatsit as proof of the customer's identity and receipt of the commission.

The registration is not binding on either side. If you don't like the look of the customer, you aren't obliged to let them across the Welcome to Dunroamin doormat. Just explain that there's been a mistake and send them back to Go (without collecting £200). You're a private hotel within the meaning of the Hotel Proprietor's

Act; The Pink Book (see Further Reading p52) has some interesting comments on turning away folk who you may consider to be undesirable. Equally, if they don't appreciate the esteemed value of your emporium, they can go back to the TIC and start again. We once had a customer who didn't like the vibes coming from our house ghost. I suspect she may have been somewhat sensitive, because she made the same excuse with several other places in the area and eventually disappeared towards pastures new.

Meanwhile, back at the TIC, the staff are taking calls from other customers who want a copy of the Where To Stay Guide, or from other TICs making forward bookings in the book-a-bed-ahead scheme. They're also answering a host of questions from tourists looking for anything from Granny's grave to the public loos, so they do get a bit busy at times. One of their greatest frustrations is when they ring a B&B to make a booking and nobody answers the phone. Another is to discover that there aren't any vacancies because the host has forgotten to inform them that they're full.

When your bookings are a bit scarce, as does happen, resist the temptation to blame the staff for not sending anyone. They're agents and are not allowed to recommend their friends before you; it's the guests who decide where they want to stay.

THE QUALITY GRADING SCHEME

Quality in Tourism administer this on behalf of Visit England, or the equivalent in Wales, Scotland and Northern Ireland. These schemes are extremely valuable in the drive towards improving the standard of accommodation in the UK of hotels and serviced accommodation: B&Bs, guest houses, farmhouses and the like. Much like sister schemes run by the AA and the RAC, they award symbols according to the facilities and quality of everything from towels to toilets to the warmth of greeting.

The Quality Assurance Scheme provides a very comprehensive list of what is expected in the way of facilities in order to qualify for different numbers of symbols. The standards for your country in the UK are available from some TICs or Quality in Tourism; the AA and RAC have parallel schemes. In England they are laid out in a booklet entitled How To Achieve the Rating You Want For Your Business – New Harmonised Standards for Serviced Accommodation in England.

Registration requires an initial inspection fee of about two room-nights. You then wait for The Inspector to stay, incognito. In the morning, after paying the bill and getting a receipt, they produce their card and sit down to give a thorough assessment of your B&B. It can be a very salutary experience to have an unbiased opinion of your product; but also a slightly unnerving one, especially if a female inspector is assessing the quality of another woman's home. However, they aren't dragons; in fact they're highly trained and incredibly tactful. Let's face it, quality assessment is quintessentially subjective; it's easy enough to count towels, but the quality of a smile is a different kettle of fish.

One inspector in Scotland had a fearful reputation for his dislike of melamine furniture and the word was that you wouldn't get a grading if you had any in your house. Fortunately, that sort of idiosyncrasy (sic) has gone out of the window with the new Harmonised Standards agreed between AA, RAC and Visit Wherever.

You don't have to join the scheme but there is a general move towards membership. In Europe, practically every type of accommodation has to be graded, and the customers are gradually becoming aware of similar schemes in the UK. Choosing a B&B can be a bit of a lottery and it will quite often boil down to availability, price, or gut feeling based on anything from a pretty name to roses round the door. Symbols signify some sort of inspection and provide a baseline of quality; my business has certainly benefited from having the top grading. I had a telephone booking from an American who was staying at the prestigious Gleneagles Hotel; he was intrigued that I had the same Quality Grading as they did and just had to come and see for himself.

ANGELA CAMPBELL

SPOT THE INSPECTOR

You can spot 'em a mile off; one person with one briefcase staying for one night and maybe wanting dinner. So you play the game of pretending that you don't know who they are, while they play the game of being a bona fide guest. I'll pretend I don't know that you know that I know, and so on. In the morning, after paying the bill, the card is presented. 'Surprise, surprise,' say you, and the inspector feels very warm inside.

I reckoned an inspector was coming to stay. I'd taken the booking but forgotten to ask him if there was anything he couldn't eat, so I dialled 1471 to call him back. He'd forgotten to block his number, so my suspicions were confirmed when I found that he lived in the next town. Over dinner the conversation skirted round his occupation as we played The Game. Eventually he put down his eating irons and said, 'Look, it's pretty obvious you know who I am, so shall we stop pretending?' Laughter melted the atmosphere and we all relaxed into a great evening talking about the B&B business.

Another one was quite different. I suspected she was up to something when I found her huddled in whispered conversation with the other guests, which stopped guiltily as I entered the room; it turned out that they had spotted her and she was trying to get them to keep schtum. It was evidently her first solo assignment; she felt she had to find something wrong to justify her inspector status. 'Don't you think it would be a good idea to rake all those fir cones off the lawn?' When I pointed out that the gale that night was responsible for the fir cones, aforesaid, she buttoned her mouth and renewed my top-quality grading.

5: GETTING THEM ACROSS THE DOORMAT

THE FRIENDLY PHONE

Back to TLC again. Here you are trawling the internet or flicking through the pages of a super glossy brochure entitled Where To Stay in Sunny Seamouth. Your eye is drawn to a lovely picture of Dunroamin, complete with smiling people admiring roses round the door. (Well done, Mrs Whatsit, you're learning.) You reach for the phone and ring to check availability. And ring. And ring. And ring. Eventually that dreaded answer machine tells you to leave a message after the beep. You say, 'Oh bother' (or some earthy Anglo-Saxon equivalent). You're the most important person on this planet and if Mrs Whatsit can't satisfy your needs right now, if not before, you'll take your esteemed custom elsewhere, won't you? So what do you do? You try Mrs Tothername on the next page, that's what you do.

One of the most difficult dividing lines to define in the B&B business is that between providing a service and letting it rule your life. It's something which only you can decide, but there is a tendency – certainly at the beginning – to try hard for business. I've been at it for 15 years and the Talking Bone is still part of my anatomy. You learn to live with it because a missed call might be a missed room-night; or a week of 'em, which is seven times as bad.

This might sound excessive but I have a landline for cost-conscious Scots and Yorkshiremen, a cordless and a mobile. The cordless comes with me to the bathroom and into the garden. When I leave the house in the winter I use the answer machine, but rarely in the high season; that's when I divert calls to the mobile and carry it wherever I go. A point to beware: British Telecom (BT) may charge you an arm and a leg to divert calls to your mobile. I get round that by leaving my mobile number on the answer machine greeting; that way, the punter picks up the tab.

I attended a training session on telephone technique, which revealed some thought-provoking ideas: the optimum time to answer is between two and five rings; leave it for the first two so that the customer can marshal their thoughts; after four, they may think you're in the pub. Just saying 'Hello' is meaningless; don't bother with the telephone number, they just want to know that they're talking to Mrs Whatsit at Dunroamin and that she really wants their business. The smile in your voice is infectious. And they want to hear yes, not no; very profound.

Two rings. Smile. Pick up the phone. 'Good morning, this is Mrs Whatsit at Dunroamin.'

THE ANSWER MACHINE

It's a constant source of astonishment to me that so many businesses don't realise how important this can be as the first point of contact. It can be (almost) as frustrating as the computer, largely because it's an open-ended communication loop, and because it often doesn't tell you what you want to know. All too often you don't even know if you've reached the right number. That wretched bossy besom from BT telling you that the person you want is out, or 'Hello, we're not in right now,' just doesn't cut the mustard. As a customer, you want to know that you've reached Dunroamin, whether they have availability and – most importantly – when they will return your call. Before I leave the house, I re-record the greeting message as cheerily and efficiently as I can. Typically, 'Hello, this is the answer machine of Campbells in Dartmouth. This week, we have availability on Monday the 7th, Tuesday and Sunday. Please try my mobile 0779 xxx xxxx or leave a message and I'll return your call as soon as possible after 11.30 a.m. Thank you.'

A WEE BIT OF SUBTLE PSYCHOLOGY

Names are the most important words in the lexicon. When a customer hears you using theirs, they come over all of a glow and they just love it. Foreign guests feel really good too, if you can manage the odd phrase in their language; a 'Guten Morgen' or a 'Bonjour' can turn a query into a booking. My old man gets round Europe with one phrase which he can trot out in five languages: two beers please and my wife will pay; breaks the ice but we seem to consume a lot of Eurobeer.

It's entirely up to you of course, but I prefer the more relaxing use of first names. Some guests, especially the more mature brethren, prefer not to use them, at least until they feel sufficiently comfortable to do so. If they don't offer theirs, I try using surnames until they ask me to do otherwise, or coax them into relaxing with some phrase like, 'Do you mind if we use first names; it's so much easier, don't you think?'

THE BOOKING BOOK

OK so the book is by the phone, pencil sharpened, smile in place and you're bright-eyed and bushy-tailed, ready to secure that first booking. What do you need to know, besides their name and the number of nights? A contact telephone number or email, and roughly what time they're planning to arrive are essential; there's nowt more frustrating than waiting in all day, just in case they turn up. If there's any doubt, one way round this problem is to ring them the day before arrival to determine if they want directions, check their estimated time of arrival and wish them a safe journey.

I also ask whether they have any special dietary needs, and how the money is to be paid; I don't accept plastic and prefer cash.

A useful detail to agree at this stage is the date when you will scrub out a provisional booking; some customers will make one and not take it up, for whatever reason. When you accept a reservation, say on a Tuesday, agree with the customer that you will assume they have changed their mind if you haven't received their deposit by Friday; three working days are more than adequate for the delivery of first-class mail. The same goes for short-term telephone bookings. Agree with them that they will arrive by, say, five o'clock so that you can re-let the room before the TIC closes. You're pretty well assured that a TIC reservation will produce the people but, again, ask when they intend to arrive so you're not waiting at their convenience.

I take dogs, so I ask for an assurance that they're clear of fleas and worms.

Finally, I ask where they heard of us.

DEPOSITS

Most Brits are used to the idea of sending a deposit, if there's time. Foreigners are not so; and don't ask for one from the Japanese because they take it as an affront to their honesty.

I've had my fingers burned enough by no-shows, so I sometimes ask for a deposit of the first-night's stay to secure the booking; you're quite at liberty to retain it if they fail to arrive. I ask for a cheque or BACS, but a credit card number can be used, providing that you have agreed the arrangement when the reservation was made.

CONFIRMATION

I email, telephone or write to confirm receipt of the deposit; don't tell my old man, but I always send it first class. I make a point of stipulating just what the rate includes: full British breakfast, parking, etc. and state what the outstanding balance will be, so that they know exactly where they stand. I had an unfortunate misunderstanding with one couple. Our rates in the Where To Stay brochure stated £25 for double occupancy. They came to stay for a week to celebrate their silver wedding anniversary. They were delightful but evidently somewhat financially challenged. When I presented the bill, they were acutely embarrassed to find that the rate was £25 per person, not per couple, which was totally unrealistic. I agonised over this awful misunderstanding and finally suggested that they pay the remaining 50% when they could. They did, but it made the point that we have to be absolutely unambiguous.

GREETING

So, comes the moment that their car is at the door. Great excitement; the pound signs leap up behind the eyeballs as the front door bell rings – money, money!

A little more psychology here. They may have had a long, frustrating drag down the motorway; probably had a row about who can't navigate to your front door; the kids are grizzling again; and Granny can't find her knitting. Let them arrive. Rather than rushing out to greet them with open arms, let them get settled and feeling comfortable. When they ring the doorbell, they're as ready for you as you are for them. They may also be feeling a little apprehensive about whether the booking arrangements have worked and if you're what they expected: will the room be ready; will Mrs Whatsit really have her teeth and curlers in, and so on. 'Ah, you must be Mr and Mrs Punter. I'm Sybil and this is my husband Basil, how nice to see you.' Warm smiles and handshakes all round works wonders.

You have about a nanosecond to make up your mind about them at this stage. As a hotel owner – sounds rather grand but it's your definition in law – you can turn them away if you doubt their ability to pay, or they're not in a fit state to be received. You've got to be pretty careful about any other reason.

SATISFACTORY

The Mini screeched to a halt on the gravel and parked on the lawn 90° across the parking line. My old man is, sometimes, quite a gent, but he had a hard job gritting his teeth at the sight of it. Out of the Mini climbed three Antipodean females of a certain age who had evidently had a hard day. As they were shown round the bedrooms, they tried all the lights and poked this and prodded that, muttering grudgingly, 'Satisfactory.'

They stayed but so did their attitude. To understate the case, they were hardly our most favourite guests; my home satisfactory, the nerve of the women! We tried to contain ourselves but just had to share the experience. A colleague down the glen was sympathetic. 'So they wound up with you; I had to throw them out.'

Two fellow guests were more supportive. They disappeared on a shopping spree and returned with a stag's head mounted on a plaque, which they presented to us with due ceremony. On the back was written, 'Thanks for a great stay. Everything was very SATISFACTORY!'

LITTLE TOUCHES

Simple courtesies, like the offer to help with their baggage and showing them to their room are really appreciated and help them to feel relaxed in someone else's home. So much better than, 'Right, you're in the back room. Here's the key. Lights out by ten o'clock. Breakfast at seven, out by eight. Any questions?' I must make a note to keep Basil chained up in the back yard when we've got company.

A Welcome to Dunroamin notice also helps: emergency and taxi telephone numbers, our address for those, where to locate us at night and Wi-Fi codes are all helpful. You should include a statement about fire equipment and evacuation.

I have a simple map of the area showing the restaurants and pubs which I can recommend; I discuss these over a Welcome-to-Dunroamin cup of tea. If we have time, I take them round the town on Campbell's Conducted Tour to show them where the places are.

Going that extra mile has been the key to getting my awards.

REGISTRATION

The government is in the process of trying to get rid of this bit of red tape; common sense rules and hopefully it's a candidate for the post-Brexit bonfire. But it's still in force. Guest registration is required by the Immigration (Hotel Records) Order 1972, as amended; just thought you'd like to know that, but I don't know anyone who sticks to the letter of this law. Broadly, guests over the age of 16 are required to register their name and nationality; foreigners also have to record the number and place of issue of their passport and, if possible, their next destination. I keep a simple card index box for these and I find it useful to have other details, like their address and phone number and date of stay. This provides a useful database for further contact, from taking future bookings to forwarding belongings left behind. If you use computer registration, you'll need to watch out for Data Protection Act requirements.

Another detail worth noting is their car numberplate; this can be useful for car parking arrangements or, heaven forbid, chasing reluctant payers.

WHO'S THE MUG?

It was getting towards the end of the season one year when we were really stung. The Assistant Boss let them in and I'm never going to let him forget it. They had come for one night and asked to stay on, wining and dining each night in the restaurant and shouting us drinks on their bill. On the fourth morning, they said that they'd be back late and could they keep the front door key. It wasn't until the following morning that we discovered we had an empty room and an unpaid bill for over £360; and of course their registration address didn't exist. If I'd been on the qui vive, a note of their car numberplate might have helped to trace them.

6: WHAT ELSE TO PROVIDE

SPACE

I wouldn't presume to tell you how to furnish and run your house – the nerve of the woman – and please don't think I'm trying to insult your intelligence. But there are sometimes some pretty obvious requirements that are often missed: one is adequate storage space for guests' clothes and enough hangers, preferably of the same pattern. Another is to leave the cupboards and drawers empty; leaving the room clear of evidence from previous occupancy is a good maxim. Put-down space for all those bits and bobs, so precious to us womenfolk, is so obvious it's often forgotten.

BITS AND BOBS

The Quality in Tourism criteria will give you a good idea of what the industry expects. I add those extras which I would like to see when I'm being pampered on a weekend away with my favourite man: face wipes, a magnifying mirror, tissues by the bed, shampoos, luxury soaps, boxes of paper tissues, a hair drier and a dressing gown. The list is almost endless, but the maxim of 'Do unto others' is a pretty good yardstick.

It's worth reiterating that you don't have to turn your home into a mini-hotel in order to get going. Nor do you have to make all the alterations at once; I managed perfectly well by opening up my home as it was and then used profits to gradually upgrade to the required standard.

BATHROOMS

En suite bathrooms are expected, with easy-clean floors, a fluffy rug and, again, plenty of put-down space.

If you need to install en-suite facilities, a shower is perfectly adequate; but if you can also fit in a bath, it will provide extra flexibility. On our travels, we've developed a bit of a phobia about showers. Top of our pet hates is the fixed faucet somewhere up near the ceiling, delivering a turgid trickle of lukewarm water, which changes temperature rapidly whenever someone flushes a loo. Or the mixer tap on the bath, which only works when pressure is put on the mounting. How much more satisfactory to have a thermostatically-protected shower, with the spray head mounted on a slider rail. We certainly appreciate the elbowroom available in an 80cm shower tray, or wider.

And somewhere to place both soap and shampoo. Don't you just hate using second-hand soap when you stay in someone else's house? Small guest soaps can be bought in boxes from the Cash and Carry or from a specialist supplier. Try Out of Eden. Tel 01768 372 939. However, these are expensive, and what do you do with all the used ones? Soap and shampoo dispensers are the norm in most hotels.

There are various combinations for providing the extra hot water; Sod's Law states that your boiler will break down just before the guests arrive. One of my bathrooms is fed from the gas combi-boiler, another from the domestic hot water cylinder. I have to grit my teeth and turn up the thermostat on the cylinder during the season; it may boost the gas bill, but it does provide enough hot water for two consecutive baths. Once we'd made a bit of dosh, we bit the bullet and installed solar thermal panels. They have an extra tank and pre-heat the cold water feed to the hot water cylinder. They've doubled our hot water capacity and really don't need sunshine to produce heat. If you have photovoltaic solar panels, there's a clever bolt-on Auto Immersion switch, which directs unused current via your hot water immersion heater en route to the grid; saves on the need for separate thermal panels.

ELECTRICS

How often do you stay somewhere and have to hunt for a socket to take the hair drier? It's usually at floor level behind the bed, just where you want it! It's a simple DIY job to run an extension, through electrical trunking, to above dressing table height where it's really needed. And, while you're at it, fit a double 13amp socket; there's always a need for more outlets.

Is there a shaver socket in the bathroom and a mirror with a light? You may not need it, but many men do.

Guests like warm towels, even in the summer. To save using central heating, I fit an electrical oil-filled radiator in each bathroom; they're reasonably inexpensive and only pull 15watts.

How often do you find a bedside lamp which provides illumination but not enough for reading? A separate reading lamp is always appreciated.

A cordless jug kettle is recommended.

Each of my bedrooms has a small radio/alarm; they cost little and many guests have said how useful they are.

They expect TV in their room; an adjustable mounting is useful so they can watch it from anywhere in the room. One of the most useful facilities on modern sets is a volume block which can be pre-programmed to a sensibly low level. We've stayed in quite a few places where we've asked how the TV works and which channels are available, only to be told, 'Oh, my husband knows about that.' Not too terribly professional, Mrs Whatsit; your man may tell you not to touch it, but you really ought to know how it works.

WE SPEND A THIRD OF OUR LIVES IN BED

It's a bit of a gamble knowing whether to provide double or twin beds. With two rooms, the optimum combination is probably to have one of each, with a zip-together mattress to join the singles; I have a foldaway single bed for extra flexibility. From what guests tell me, the general preference is for firm mattresses. My local furnisher supplies commercial Contract mattresses at very competitive prices. A good quality mattress topper with a waterproof cover is worth having. I provide two pillows for each guest: one feather and one synthetic, both with an internal cover.

Most guests are happy with duvets; it's worth having both summer and winterweight ones if you can. In summer, guests like to have two sheets so they can chuck off the duvet if they get too hot.

I provide each guest with a bath towel, a hand towel and a flannel. To avoid confusion, I supply a set in different colours for each guest in the room. The greatest amount of wear and tear is to bedding and towels, especially when they have to be washed after every one-night stay.

And do remember to supply a spare loo roll in the bathroom.

Guests appreciate a tea/coffee tray in their bedroom. I loathe those awful plastic containers of UHT milk and provide a jug or flask of fresh milk. We stayed in a B&B where a small fridge was available outside the bedroom; their fans are often too noisy for inside. I also supply a selection of biscuits and a bottle of filtered water.

SKIMMED MILK

She arrived late on a Saturday night, long after the shops had shut. As I showed her the room, I explained that a flask of fresh milk for the tea tray would be outside her door first thing in the morning. 'I only drink tea with skimmed milk,' said she, all nonchalant-like as if skimmed milk was the norm in the depths of darkest Devon.

It only rains at night here, or so the brochures will have you believe, but it did the next morning. In bucketfuls. My dear old man donned his wellies and sloshed down town to get Madam her skimmed milk. 'Damned inconsiderate,' he muttered through slightly-clenched teeth. 'Might just have told us when she booked the room; service is bloody service, I suppose.' Not really an early morning man, bless him.

She got her special milk, which was proudly in place for Madam's delectation at breakfast.

'Oh,' said she, 'I only drink coffee with semi-skimmed milk.' The smile grew just a mite thinner; was she trying to wind us up or was she an inspector?

My Front of House man went through the menu: free range local eggs cooked any which way, crispy bacon, delicious local sausages bursting with herbs, homemade bread and marmalade, etc. A glaze crept into Madam's eyes. 'I'm vegetarian and I only eat eggs with cheese.'

At this point, he suffered a serious sense of humour failure. Teeth ground. 'Oh dear, we appear to be fresh out of cheese.' She had toast. And she didn't bloody well return!

THE MOST IMPORTANT MEAL OF THE DAY

My old man has stayed in a lot of hotels (usually in four-star internationals, the rat) and he has a bee in his bonnet about breakfasts. There must be a minimum of: fruit juice, fresh fruit, yoghurt, cereals with milk and bread on the sideboard. I always ask the guests when they want their toast and coffee. I was most impressed by one B&B owner who offered three different strengths of coffee; and another who had a large selection of teas.

No self-respecting chef will get out of his bed to cook breakfast, so it's usually left to lesser mortals; and all too often, it's Mrs Mop wot comes in and does. It's pretty obvious when bacon and sausages have been left in the oven overnight, and my man reckons that a Bain Marie full of rubbery scrambled eggs is an invention of the culinary devil.

Guests appreciate a choice, rather than having the compulsory British Fry with black pudding and deep-fried haggis, plonked down in front of them; you'll finish it or I'll let your tyres down. I hate waste because it's one of the greatest drains on profit, so I don't pre-cook anything; they really appreciate freshly-cooked food served straight from the pan on warm plates. They don't mind in the least waiting 10 minutes while I cook for them, because that's all it takes. Mark you, when four guests want one poached egg, one scrambled, one boiled and one fried, all with different combinations of bacon, sausage mushrooms and tomato, I'm working like two one-armed paper hangers. This type of order can be cooked all at once on a domestic cooker with four rings and a grill; my microwave is a godsend.

We have a bee in our bonnets about 'Hands up who's having…?' in any eatery. Very unprofessional; it's so easy to make a note of who wants what, so you put the right food in front of the right guest without asking.

I stock mustards and funny-coloured sauces as a service.

RIGHT LUV, WHERE'S THE BROWN SAUCE?

A spot of mustard is fine, but when he asked for the brown sauce I felt that the subtle flavours of my culinary creation were being somewhat insulted.

'Brown sauce? I use that for cleaning brass. Have you any idea what that stuff does to your insides?'

'Aye, love. It cleans 'em out right proper. Now where's the brown sauce?'

Portion control is second only to paper and plastic on my restaurant hate list. We were most impressed by the attitude of a restaurateur we visited, way back before we started our hotel. When we asked for a glass of sherry as an aperitif, he brought the bottle and left it on the table with a big bowl of olives. I love olives. Before we paid, he asked if we had drunk more than one glass of sherry each. OK, so he probably charged us for a half bottle, but the trust he placed in us and the Horn-of-Plenty approach, so impressed us that we went back to that restaurant time and again. We carried that philosophy into our restaurant and now I continue with it in the B&B. They rarely make pigs of themselves; they really appreciate a bowl of butter balls and a jar of marmalade on the table and a tin of assorted biscuits in their room, instead of those tight-fisted penny-pinching sachets one finds in most hotels. I like to provide freshly baked bread when possible; wake up and smell the bread! Guests are quite happy to carve their own slices. I cut any leftovers and shove individually-wrapped slices in the freezer for toast; they thaw in the toaster.

Linen napkins add a touch of quality.

Some guests are just not morning people, but I've found they quite like sitting around our dining table making conversation; mine is a home and how many homes have separate breakfast tables? But that really does depend on what ambiance you prefer.

And they're usually happy to have breakfast from 8.30. I started by asking when they wanted to eat; after all, it's their holiday. But I really got stung when someone said 5.30 because he had to catch the red-eye special from the airport. I found him sitting reading the paper at 10.00. 'I was just testing to see if you meant it.' I wiped the floor with him and chucked him out. The very cheek of him.

Quality shows. There may be a tendency, at least to begin with, to settle for less than the best. But the philosophy of 'It'll do, it's only for the guests' really does get noticed; they may not say anything to you, apart from voting with their feet.

WASH YOUR FEET

I do a spot of gardening. It helps to grow one's own fruit and vegetables; gets me out of the house and is thoroughly therapeutic. Kitchen and garden waste is composted and I used to supplement that with a fertiliser called Dug, which is made from chicken litter and has a rather pungent pong. A lady guest had a bit of a problem with her feet. One morning she came down to breakfast looking rather embarrassed; she'd washed her feet three times but still couldn't get rid of the smell. You've guessed it. After that, I stopped putting Dug on the flowerbed outside the bedroom windows.

MAINTENANCE

Checking that everything works regularly is pretty bloomin' obvious, but checking that all the lights work when you're cleaning the rooms in daylight is easily overlooked. And how many hoteliers fail to observe the most elementary rule of sleeping in all their bedrooms, at least once, in order to really sample their products? One B&B owner we visited had a notice asking guests to check that she hadn't forgotten to switch on the water heater; not too terribly professional!

7: MONEY, MONEY

HOW MUCH TO CHARGE

The question of how much to charge is not as difficult as it may seem. Just check out the competition and make your own value judgement. Somebody once told me that the key to business success is to believe in your product, devote all your energy towards it, and to charge a bit more than your competitors. It may sound a bit daft, but it works.

Your accountant will allow you to charge the cost of breakfast against income. The recommended way is to list every single ingredient: one sausage, two slices of bacon, a tomato, etc., plus VAT if you've got that far, and add it all up. When we started running our restaurant, the Assistant Boss – who, for all his faults, is no slouch when it comes to business – went through that exercise precisely twice. He took one look at it and realised that the market just wouldn't accept the result; it was too low. So we charged what we thought was the acceptable rate. Our wine list was pretty modestly priced but there were three which were deliberately priced-up, to attract the credit-credibility of the customers; there were always one or two who just had to choose the most expensive wine so they could swank to their wives or mistresses.

ACCOUNTS

It's really quite simple to keep basic trading accounts. A lot of small businesses go to the wall for lack of willingness to do this essential task; they're too busy doing their job to scrape a living. Receipts get stuffed into a shoe box 'for later'; later becomes later and before they know it the Inland Revenue are on their backs.

Come on, this is all getting a bit maudlin, ain't it? It's not that bad. All it requires is a simple system for keeping track of what comes in and what goes out and the determination to sit down, say once a month, to write up the books. And it really is worth doing.

You may think that Mrs Whatsit down the road shoves all that dosh into her back pocket and doesn't tell the tax man. But you don't really know. Once you start advertising, someone will know what you're doing: whether it's that old busybody behind the twitching curtains across the street or the man in the plain van, it makes no difference. Sooner or later they will want to know; and if they get a sniff of tax evasion, they'll be down on you like two tons of bricks.

Tax avoidance is not only legal, it's smart. The great advantage of having an accountant is that tax avoidance is what he's about. He knows the rules and he knows the shortcuts. For example: I charge the business a standard amount for running to the supermarket in the car each week; and all the rates and energy bills and telephone and insurance and cleaner's wages go into the accounts. And it's all perfectly legal.

You don't even have to be good at numbers; I was an absolute dunderhead at maths in school and even I can do it. Your accountant will deal with the tedium of adding up the totals; he'll have to do it anyway, so don't bother. He will probably charge you in relation to the amount of work he does, so you can keep his bill down by doing your own trading accounts.

It doesn't require anything high-tech; a stubby pencil and a rubber will do just fine. I have a money box – no, not a piggy bank, just a tin box – a receipt book and a spike made from a knitting needle poked through a bit of wood. All receipts go on the spike until I do the accounts at the end of the month; the receipt book is used for the window cleaner and the very occasional guest who wants one; and the tin box is for hiding in the sock drawer where the kids can't find it.

A lot of folk use a spreadsheet or computer program. I keep my accounts on a set of loose-leaf cash column sheets, but there are lots of different types of book available in the stationers. All business-related receipts are cross-referenced, which just means that I write 1 on the first one, 2 on the second and so on. In the cash column, that number is entered to show what it's for. Unless it's absolutely obvious, it's worth making a note on the top of each receipt what it's about before it gets stuck on the spike; you may think you'll remember, but a month's a long time to stretch the memory bank. The value of doing this is enormous, not least because it means less work for the accountant, which means his bill is less, which means my old man hasn't gone too bald over the years.

All records have to be kept for the set period, currently six years, so they go into the attic after the tax man has agreed the accounts. One of the world's big spenders, I splash out and have a separate shoe box for each year's receipts.

Another advantage of keeping accounts is that you can figure out how you're doing at the end of each trading year, and year on year. In general, the greatest profit margin will come from bedrooms, followed by evening meals.

BANKING

The bank knows I run a wee B&B and they're quite happy to let me use my private account, which is free; just ask them what they charge for a business account.

To take plastic or not to take plastic, that is the question. I resent paying four per cent for the privilege and I've never lost a booking because I can't process the stuff, but it can be useful if you have a lot of rooms. I lost money in bank charges once when I accepted a Euro cheque over the stipulated maximum and conversion rates frighten the hell out of me. Most of my guests are quite happy to pay cash, given a bit of notice; I've never had a rubber cheque yet, touch wood.

Running a business is an entree to trade prices for a whole range of goods and services; I don't bother with Cash and Carry, but some folk swear by them. A business card is a useful tool when negotiating for a better price.

LAUNDRY

This can take up a hell of a lot of time, especially with one-night stays. OK, so you want to save as much money as possible – especially to begin with – but what price is your time? There are companies who specialise in the hotel trade. They will provide all your linen, take it away for laundering and leave you with replacements. Others will just do the washing and ironing. Alternatively, if you can't cope with ironing sheets and duvet covers, you may be lucky enough to find an ironing-only service; mine takes it away on Monday and returns it on Wednesday. Given that most business is at weekends, this is a boon. And the cost is tax-deductible. Wear and tear on the washing machine and tumble drier is another thing altogether.

PARTNERS

One of the soundest bits of business advice I had was only to take a partner who is either your bank manager or your husband; I took my husband on because he had an honest face and I felt sorry for him; besides, he's a tax advantage.

NO-SHOWS

If guests fail to arrive without telling you, you've got a problem. A deposit of the first-night's stay helps to bridge that gap. If all else fails, you can take them to the Small Claims Court for breach of contract. Procedures are a doddle; they don't cost much and you can claim that back, plus interest at an attractive rate, when you win. You should wait until the end of the contract period and must make every effort to re-let the room. Quite often a letter threatening action will produce the money, especially when you point out that the claim will be increased by court costs. The best you can hope for is two-thirds of the value of the booking, plus costs.

THINGS LEFT BEHIND

Guests often leave things in the room. It's easy enough to dispose of the odd bottle of shampoo, but anything more valuable can pose a few problems on both sides; I nearly won a fur coat once but, sadly, she came back a week later to claim it! There are no regulations that I can find which covers this, so common decency dictates that one should make every effort to track down the owner; hence the value of registration cards.

HAS ANYONE SEEN FRED'S TOOTH?

The body language was all too obvious. They'd lost something. Up and down the stairs they went, out to the car, back up the stairs; it went on for half an hour before they swallowed their embarrassment and asked if we'd found Fred's tooth. He had to wear it in the office; when on holiday he would leave it in a glass on the bathroom shelf. She had one too, just like Fred's, which she took out to show us. It was minute, just one small ersatz molar on a bit of pink plastic.

And then it dawned on me. When I'd cleaned their bathroom that morning there was a bit of water in the tooth glass which I'd chucked down the loo, as one does. Unfortunately, there had gone Fred's tooth. Poor Fred, but it does you good to have a laugh. Unfortunately, the last laugh was on me; they shot off back to London to get another tooth, leaving me with an empty room for the night.

EVEN MORE SUBTLE PSYCHOLOGY

Money can destroy relationships quicker than lightning, especially with staff. So, I hold the tin box and nobody else gets their sticky little fingers into it. It's such a sensitive subject that we don't even joke about it with the guests. I used to hate asking for money, but I grew out of that pretty damn quickly; and counting it out in front of the guests after they've paid still gives me the heebie-jeebies. Apart from the deposit, we found that the mutually comfortable plan is to leave it 'til they're good and ready. If they offer to pay upfront, take the money and run; they may get knocked down by a bus the next minute. Otherwise, read the body language; somebody will usually start fishing around in pockets or purses or wallets right after breakfast. And that's the time to ask them if everything was all right. Quite often I've wanted to point out some problems – or even to make a wee complaint – but haven't had the opportunity because the hostess was so nice. I usually offer a receipt but, apart from window cleaners, businessmen and Inspectors, they rarely want one.

SO, WHAT'S IT WORTH?

So now for the nitty gritty; how much can you expect to make in a year? The answer is about the same as the length of a piece of string. It depends on your location, how much you charge, the length of the season, the weather, the strength of the pound, the World Cup and all. The problem is that you know why guests come, but not why they don't; it's almost impossible to answer the imponderable. My, we are getting deep. However, if you charge £100 per night for a double room, it's probably about right to work on a net £3,500 per room in a four-month season, once you're up and running. Don't bank on it and for goodness sake don't sue me if it doesn't work out, but does that help? Bear in mind that it may take three seasons to build up the business.

8: YOU CAN'T PLEASE ALL THE FOLK ALL THE TIME

This business is essentially about pleasing customers and providing what they want when they need it, within reason. Your approach is the key: if you like people and let them know that you value their custom, this will be a doddle; if you treat them as milch cows, they'll soon sense that and not return – they may even walk out on you. That's not to say that you've got to prostitute yourself, or roll over on your back wagging your tail at their beck and call; they are guests in your home, albeit paying ones. I like to treat them as if they are the best friends of a favourite relative and I find that works extremely well. There will be some who won't understand the relationship, or try to take advantage of your hospitality. But, let's face it, they're in as strange a relationship with you as you are with them; there are bound to be some misunderstandings initially.

BUT I DON'T LIKE NUTS

My choccie pud was a firm favourite in the restaurant. The menu quite clearly stated Dark Chocolate Mousse with brandy and cream, topped with nuts. The last serving went into the restaurant and almost immediately returned. 'The lady says she doesn't like nuts.'

We were coming towards the end of one of those long, hot and perspiry summer evenings when the staff were suffering the butt end of my sense of humour failure. I didn't realise that the swing door into the dining room was not completely shut. 'What's wrong with the woman? Nuts it says and nuts she's bloody well got.' A short time later, the swing door eased open and a face appeared. 'I'm the bloody woman who doesn't like nuts,' she said, 'I think your chocolate mousse was delicious and I've come to pay the bill.' We all collapsed into embarrassed laughter, but from thenceforth the cry would go round the kitchen, (sotto voce) 'Door opening. Wife, button your mouth!'

COMPLAINTS

If you have a good experience you tell four people; have a bad one and you'll tell 14. The best time to deal with this is before they leave.

I had a letter of complaint once, passed on through the TIC. My immediate reaction was 'What have I done? It's all my fault and the business will go down the drain. Doom, gloom, sell the kids and move into the workhouse.' After a stiff whisky, I realised that the complainant had a point, however minor. So I wrote to him explaining the situation and naively enclosed a rebate. His reply was that it just proved I was guilty. Oh boy, there was one professional whinger who won't get into my house again.

FOREIGNERS

Cultural differences can provide some interesting experiences. Tipping is one of those imponderables which can confuse even the most experienced travellers, but the Assistant Boss was quite surprised to get a £1 tip for carrying a Japanese guest's bag. Give them a wee bow when you meet them and, if they offer their business card, take it with both hands and read it appreciatively. And don't count their money in front of them; they consider that an affront to their honesty.

North Americans tend to forget the importance to us of Please and Thank You; it's just their way, but I do have to bite my tongue when they don't use those magic words.

A German once spoke to me as a servant. 'You vill get me medicine.' I reckoned he just didn't understand; after all, how's your command of colloquial German?

Arabs can consider it rude to shake hands while sitting. My, we're really becoming quite the International Host of the Year, aren't we?

NOISES

I was showing a rather timid couple their room. They were rather confused about the rhythmic noises coming through the party wall accompanied by squeals of delight. Had they come to some sort of knocking shop? They were a might mollified when I suggested that the others were evidently trying to procreate their nation without much success!

STRANGERS IN YOUR HOME

It's a gamble allowing strangers into your home: you just don't know who you're going to get. Yorkshire men will tell you that there's nowt as daft as folk. There was the man who just wandered into my home without so much as a knock on the door, straight into my bedroom as I was changing, and asked for a room. And the German who demanded that I get his companion a prescription for cystitis. And the guests who said they'd arrive at four o'clock but didn't turn up till ten o'clock at night, which left us wondering whether they'd arrive at all.

As they stand on the doormat, you have about 30 seconds to decide whether you want them; you will soon develop a sixth sense about that. One of my greatest mistakes was to almost reject a couple in motorbike leathers; they turned out to be two of the most delightful Scandawegians, touring Scotland on a Goldwing. The TIC staff can act as a filter, especially if they've seen around your home beforehand.

There will be times when you resent strangers in your home, especially at the beginning of the season. I find that a privacy zone – our sitting room – is a must, and an occasional day without guests is hugely beneficial.

WILL THEY PINCH THE SILVER?

Your family may misuse your belongings but paying guests will abuse them; I've had it up to here with wet towels left on beds and on the back of antique chairs; guests have broken chairs and tables and keys and towel rails by just being plain thoughtless.

Apart from a few clothes hangers, I've had very few things pinched; but perhaps I've just been lucky. The worst event was when we allowed a family group free rein. 'Just treat the place as your own.' And they did. It wasn't until the following Christmas that we failed to find the half case of Grand Cru which had been stored in a cupboard. OK, we'd brought it abroad and it didn't cost very much, but the abuse of our hospitality really hurt.

But quite honestly, they are the tiny minority; probably less than half of one per cent. The rest are absolutely delightful and I've found that, on the whole, they appreciate and return the trust I put in them. They come as strangers and leave as friends; we've made many firm friends over the years. One of the side effects is when they ask you back to stay, which is a trifle awkward after they've paid to stay with you. Another are your relatives and friends wanting to stay in the high season, robbing you of your bread and butter; so there's another decision you will have to make.

Insurance companies aren't daft. They know there's a possibility of paying guests making off with the valuables, and they cover themselves. You can buy a commercial policy which will cover against loss of earnings, but I don't have one as we're not doing B&B as a main business.

FINALLY

Well, I guess that's about it. I hope this has given you a good insight to the B&B business. If I haven't put you off altogether, it's a small miracle. If you're encouraged to give it a try, I wish you the best of good fortune and may the Great God Mammon smile forever upon your doormat.

FURTHER READING

The Pink Book which covers the legislation affecting serviced accommodation (that's you); there are about 33 different sections. If the TIC haven't got one go to www.visitbritain.org/pink-book, or call 0207 578 1400. It costs about £12.

ABOUT THE AUTHOR

Angela Campbell

After serving in the Women's Royal Naval Service Angela married her Royal Marine. She followed him with their two children for 27 house moves. She started doing B&B within days of moving into a lodge in Aberdeenshire. She had never done anything like it before and just put a blackboard outside the door advertising B&B Good Food; within the hour, the first guests were at the door. Almost immediately she was doing evening meals and a few years later the house was voted Best Bed and Breakfast in Scotland by the Kellogg Corporation. Her husband was declared medically unfit to continue his profession, so they converted part of their house into a wee hotel. In two years they had turned a £9,000 a year B&B into a £73,000 a year enterprise. They moved to Devon, started doing B&B again, and were voted Best Accommodation in the South Hams area in 1999 and 2001. She and her husband ran courses on How to Run a Successful B&B for retiring service personnel.

Sadly, Angela succumbed to cancer in 2012. Colin started afresh in 2014. Campbells has held the prestigious AA 5 Star rating with special Breakfast Award and listing in Alistair Sawday's Special Places to stay. It was voted best B&B for 2017 by Living in the Shires and Aspire magazines.